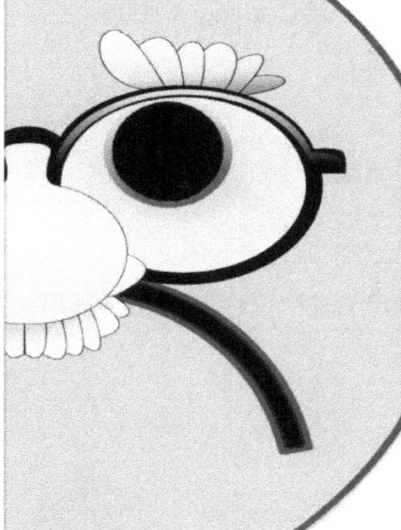

M.J. Gallagher
Let's Make A Scene!

Short Plays and Scenes for Grade School Performers

Let's Make a Scene! Short Plays and Scenes for Grade School Performers © 2014, M.J. Gallagher

Published by Mighty Gargoyle Media

ISBN   978-1-312-38761-4

All rights reserved.

All characters are fictitious and any resemblance to persons living or deceased is purely coincidental.

Djinn Rummage Original copyright 2002

All that Glitters Original copyright 2003

Candy is Dandy Copyright 2014

Cindy Claus Versus the Easter Bunny Original Copyright 1998

Birdbrains Original Copyrights 2001, 2002

Cover design by the author.

To contact the author, please e-mail mighty_gargoyle@yahoo.com

Visit www.mightygargoyle.com

Table of Contents

INTRODUCTION AND AUTHOR'S NOTE	**5**
GLOSSARY OF TERMS USED IN PLAYMAKING	**7**
DJINN RUMMAGE	**9**
ALL THAT GLITTERS	**19**
CANDY IS DANDY	**35**
CINDY CLAUS VERSUS THE EASTER BUNNY	**51**
BIRDBRAINS	**59**
EPISODE 1: "FIELD TRIP"	60
EPISODE 2: "BUGS"	72
EPISODE 3: "PIE"	79

Introduction and Author's Note

We love to play. We love to make plays!

When I was in school, I was fortunate to have many teachers who introduced us to the world of playmaking. We went to see plays, performed in school plays, read plays for fun, and listened to audio plays. Growing up with my sisters and cousisn, we often put on our own productions just for fun, too.

Playmaking is a **craft**. The result is collaborative project, and putting on a play takes a group of people. No one person can do it alone. A play is something you build with your friends! As an actor, director, teacher and playwright I've approached playmaking from a number of different perspectives. Rereading the pieces I've selected for this collection, I've decided that these scripts can be considered a recipe that you can use as a starting point for making your scene. The number of characters vary from play to play, but even if there are just two characters speaking, you'll ask yourself: Who'll direct it? Where will we get the costumes and the props? How will we create the sound effects? Who's going to turn on and off the lights?

If you're a teacher, feel free to use these scripts in your class. I wrote some of these scripts to be used in my acting classes and some to be performed for audiences.

Play scripts are fantastic tools for teaching
- Collaboration and group interaction
- Creativity and personal expression
- Responsibility
- Technical skills
- The use of language, including English as a second language
- An so much more!

Or, you can...just make a scene for fun!

About the Author

M.J. Gallagher is a cartoonist, playwright, and prose author.
As cartoonist, he is the creator of The Mystery Girls comic strip. His plays *include Cindy Claus Saves Christmas, Fast Times at Holiday High, One Lucky Night*, to name a few.

His fairy and folk tales were first collected in New Magic (2002).
A former professional actor, for three years he toured as the Host of the Recycle Rex show. He has taught acting styles that include monologues, auditioning, acting for commercials and on camera situation comedy acting.

Other Books Available by the Author

Cindy Claus Saves Christmas (Script)

Fast Times at Holiday High (Script)

Getting Lucky (Script)

The Wish-Bird, an Island Fantasy

The Jade Green Heart

Oliva & the Willow

Glossary of Terms Used in Playmaking

Act	1) To perform on stage!
	2) Plays are often broken into large sections called Acts, and contain several Scenes.
Backstage	The area behind the stage, often hidden by a wall or curtains.
Black Box	A kind of flexible studio theatrewhere the audience and actors are in the same room, and the audience may surround the players while they perform.
Blackout	Turning off or fading out stage lighting.
Block/Blocking	Arranging moves made by characters, usually noted by the Director.
Cross	To move across the stage.
CUE	1) A command technical crew to carry out a particular operation (lighting; sound).
	2) Any signal (spoken line, action) given on stage to a character that indicates another action should follow.
Discover	When the play starts, what is Discovered is what is already present on stage.
Downstage	The area of the stage closed to the audience.
Exit	1) To leave the stage.
	2) The direction in which a character leaves the stage.
EXT.	Exterior, used to indicate someplace outdoors.
FADE IN.	At the beginning of a scene, coming out of blackness on camera.
FADE OUT.	At the end of a scene, going into blackness on camera.
House	The audience or auditorium.
House Left	From the perspective of the audience, the left hand side.
House Right	From the perspective of the audience, the right hand side.
INT.	Interior, indicating the inside of a building.
Offstage	The area that is not on stage, often an action that occurs in the play, but not on stage.
Procenium Arch	The "the picture frame " of the stage, the

	Procenium is the opening which stands between stage and auditorium; can be real or imagined
Running Time	How long the play should take to be performed.
Scene	Part of a script that makes up a chapter of the script. Should tell its own story.
SFX.	Sound Effects
Stage	The area where the players put on their show!
Stage Direction	Notes made in a script that tells the Characters what they should be doing.
Stage Left	From the perspective of the players, the left hand side.
Stage Manager	During performance, the Stage Manager runs the production, telling the technical crew when to light lights, etc.
Stage Right	From the perspective of the players, the right hand side.
Upstage	The part of the stage furthest from the audience.
V.O.	Voice Over, an unseen voice.

DJINN RUMMAGE

Number of Characters: 8 Speaking parts, plus enemble. Running Time: About 20 minutes.

Self-centered Doreen finds an old magic lamp at a rummage sale, When I genie emerges from it, Doreen thinks all her dreams will come true...but that's not exactly how things turn out!

Characters:
Doreen
Sam, her friend
The Djinn, Servant of the Lamp
Rabid Fan
Biggest Fan
Disappointed Fan
Moon Leader
Moon Creatures

Setting: A rummage sale.

A large table stands just right of center, covered in doodads, crafts, clothing, toys, and the detritus of someone's life.

Two kids enter, DOREEN and SAM. Both are dressed in "thrift store chic." Sam carries a large goody bag.

Doreen sifts through the stuff on the table unceremoniously.

Doreen:
Gawd. This stuff is all crap.
Sam:
But you love rummage sales.
Doreen:
Yeah, but where's the treasure? This is just other people's junk. There's never any treasure anymore.
Sam:
Yeah, all the good stuff's been taken.
Doreen:

It's like you have to get up at five a.m. before all the antique dealers get-- *(Spying a copper pot underneath a pile)* Ooohh... what's this?
        Sam:
It looks old.
        Doreen:
Yeah, ancient.
        Sam:
Like from the seventies or something.
        Doreen:
I thought it was an old planter, but it kind of looks like a teapot.
        Sam:
It's kind of strange for a teapot.
        Doreen:
Who's the treasure hunting expert here? Look, it's a teapot. I wonder how much she wants for it.
        Sam:
Gosh, it's awfully dirty.
        Doreen:
(Commandingly) Treasure cleaning kit. *(Sam pulls out a small pouch from the goody bag and hands it to Doreen. Doreen pulls out a chamois polishing cloth from it. She begins to polish the object.)* I bet I can get it for a dollar. Let's just see what it looks like under some of this dust....

As Doreen polishes the object, fog swirls around the stage and the lights change to green and purple hues. Both Sam and the table disappear slowly into the fog and offstage.

In their place a small person appears, dressed in little else than green and purple vest, pantaloons, and slippers. The creature moves oddly, slowly and fluidly, as if made of liquid and having difficulty getting its limbs to remain stationary.

        Djinn:
Greetings and felicitations, O Great Mistress.
        Doreen:
What the —? Who are —? Where am —???
        Djinn:
You have the great fortune of releasing, for a time, the Servant of the Lamp, O My Mistress.
        Doreen:
Lamp? Ha ha ha ha ha! Oh, I get it! Great joke, Sam! Sam? Come on out now, Sam....
        Djinn:
   The Wishes thou now hast Number in three
    Ask what thou wilt To set me free
        Doreen:

Where'd all this smoke come from?

Djinn:

All that you see comes from my existence between the different worlds.

Doreen:

Okay, this is totally crazy. You are so goofin'.

Djinn:

A Servant of the Lamp endeavors only to serve, not "goof," O Mistress.

Doreen:

Okay, let me see if I get this... This...this thing is a lamp.

Djinn:

And old and precious doorway between all that there is and all that there could be.

Doreen:

Yeah, yeah, whatever. And you're the genie of the lamp....

Djinn:

Your powers of observation are beyond par with those of the most learned scholars of old, Great Mistress.

Doreen:

You were saying something about wishes.

Djinn:

For payment, this servant which you have set free
Will grant thee wishes the number of three

Doreen:

No way.

Djinn:

Way, O Great Mistress.

Doreen:

I don't believe you. You can't prove it.

Djinn:

Look around you! Where do you think—can it be that you actually doubt my powers to distort time and space to my very bidding?? I am a DJINN, spirit of the Fifth House of Amethyst and Jade! Your life is but a spark to my roaring flame! You have barely begun to learn to walk upright and yet—*(calming down)* of course the Great Mistress requires proof. It is proof she shall have. *(Waving arms in a strange fluid motion)* ABUL KELAH!

Partitions open up behind the pair to reveal a large rear-projection screen. Slides appear upon the screen to evidence the vast powers under the Djinn's control. The first slide shows an underwater scene, replete with whales and exotic fishes.

Doreen:

It's, like, a TV.

Djinn:

It is a window into the worlds I can offer you, O Mistress. Behold! All the creatures under the oceans could be yours to command, should you so desire.

Doreen:

I don't want to talk to fish.

The next few slides appear, showing the expanse of the galaxy, moving from planet to planet.

Djinn:

Great Mistress, you could traverse the Universe, exploring the wonders of all the known worlds...

Doreen:

Uh-hunh.... Okay, what else have you got?

The next slides display a fortune in jewels and gold.

Djinn:

The standard first wish is for riches beyond imagining.

Doreen:

I like that!

Djinn:

I thought you would.

Doreen:

Would I get a big house—like a mansion?

Djinn:

Of course.

Doreen:

And be driven around in a huge limousine?

Djinn:

Naturally.

Doreen:

Oh, I'd love to be rich...but not just rich. I want to be famous, too, and have people recognize and adore me wherever I go—just like a movie star!

Djinn:

Do you so rich it? I mean, wish it?

Doreen:

I do!!

Djinn:

As you have wished it, it shall be so! ABUL KELAH!

Once again waving arms strangely, causing the set to change into Rodeo Drive in L.A. Doreen pulls off her sweatshirt to reveal a fashionable top, and pulls off her jeans to reveal a trendy skirt. Sunglasses suddenly adorn her head.

Doreen:
Wow! Look at all this! No more rummage sales for me! Where are we?

Djinn:
Beverly Hills.

Doreen:
Wait till everyone back home sees this! Let's go shopping!
A Rabid Fan walks up.

Rabid Fan:
Omigaw— You-- you... do you know who you are?!?

Doreen:
Well, yeah, I—

Rabid Fan:
Doreen Markham! You're Doreen Markham!!!

Doreen:
I am?

Djinn:
Lefkowitz wasn't getting you anywhere so you changed your name to Markham.

Rabid Fan:
I love you!!! Can I have your autograph?

Doreen:
Sure. Anything for a fan! I don't know if I have a pen...

Rabid Fan:
(Calling off stage) Hey, everyone! It's Doreen Markham!!! Over here!
Several more rabid fans rush the stage, surrounding Doreen. They take pictures of her, flashing the light in her face, and scream at her. They begin to pull at her clothing, which comes off in Velcroed® strips.

Fans:
We love you, Doreen!

Biggest Fan:
I'm your biggest fan!
Disappointed Fan:
No, I am!!!

Biggest Fan:
This is so exciting!

Rabid Fan:
I need a souvenir of meeting you!
The Fans begin to beat her down to the ground.

Doreen:

Hey—What are you— OW! That's my hair! OW! Stop that! Get off me! Genie! Genie!!!! OW!!!

The Djinn steps up and waves her arms. All the Fans freeze in place.

Djinn:

DAMU TABOULAH!

The Fans slowly spread out and fade from stage, revealing a Doreen in tattered clothing, which resembles rags. Her hair is atrocious.

Biggest Fan:

Wow, I can't believe I got to meet Doreen Markham.

Disappointed Fan:

She wasn't as nice in person as I thought she would be.

Rabid Fan:

Look, I got some of her hair!

The Fans exit.

Doreen:

Look... look at me. The clothes aren't even good enough for a rummage sale now!

Djinn:

You can buy more, now that you are rich and famous.

Doreen:

I hate being famous! If this is what it's like, I hate it! I hate it!!!

Djinn:

(Helping her to her feet) Oh, you haven't given it a chance.

Doreen:

(rubbing her leg) Ow... I think one of them bit me.

Djinn:

Another wish perhaps, O Mistress?

Doreen:

People just suck! How could they do that to someone? I need to get away from everyone. I wish I could live on the Moon or something.

Djinn:

As you have wished it, it shall be so. ABUL KELAH!!

Once again, fog rises on stage, as Doreen is transformed into a space alien, with blue tentacled headdress and a blue alien outfit.

The background slide changes to that of the Moon's surface.

Doreen:

Now wait a minute! I... *(She begins to bounce around on the Moon's surface.)* Hey, this is kinda cool. It's really peaceful here.

Djinn:

(Putting on suntan lotion) Many people in the Solar System find the Moon to be the ideal vacation spot.

Doreen:
How come I can breathe and talk up here?

Djinn:
You have adapted to your environment.
Doreen inspects her body.

Doreen:
Eewwwwwww! AAAAHHH! What have you done to me! I have— tentacles growing out of my head!!!!

Djinn:
They create the portable atmosphere that allows you to breathe and speak. And, if I may say so, they are rather fetching on you, O My Mistress.

Doreen:
Blue. You've made me... blue.

Djinn:
It is the natural color of the Moon creatures, Great Mistress.

Doreen:
(Pointing through the house) They're not blue.
Three Moon Creatures, in similar costume to Doreen's but in vibrant red, enter through the house, jibbering and gesturing excitedly. The Leader waves a ray gun.

Djinn:
Well, nobody's perfect.

Moon Creatures:
Jib! Jib! Bleetak krig! Jib!

Doreen:
Greetings. Uh, we mean you no harm. Uh...take me to your... leader?

Moon Leader:
(Menacingly) Jib! Bleetak! Bleetak Krig! Jib-jib!!
The other two Moon Creatures advance on Doreen.

Doreen:
Oh, no, not this again!
The Moon Leader fires at Doreen's feet, which cause her to jump in slow motion.

Moon Leader:
(making ray gun sound effect with mouth) BRZZZZZZZRT! Jab kree... Bleetak! JIB! Jib-jib!!

The other Moon Creatures grab Doreen by each arm and begin a game of slow-motion tug of war with her.

                    Doreen:
Genie, you screw-up! This wish isn't any better than the first one. In fact, it's worse! Do something!
                    Djinn:
DAMU TABOULAH!

The three Moon Creatures "float" away.

                    Doreen:
How long have you been at this wish-and-genie game, anyway?
                    Djinn:
Ten thousand seasons have passed since first I became the Servant who travels through the portal of the Lamp, O Great Mistress.
                    Doreen:
Well, you aren't very good at it.
                    Djinn:
Perhaps you would like to take some time to reflect before making your next wish....
                    Doreen:
I mean, you have all these powers, right? You can go anywhere, do anything. How hard could it be to grant three little wishes?
                    Djinn:
Well, there are of course all the quantum calculations... folding time and space...
                    Doreen:
(Not listening) I bet even I could do a better job! And, I'd be able to do anything I want.
                    Djinn:
(Not listening) ...then of course one must keep up with the current crazes and trends....
                    Doreen:
No one would hassle me.
                    Djinn:
You sort of have to be a psychologist and personal shopper, all rolled into one.
                    Doreen:
All right. I wish it.
                    Djinn:
Wish what?
                    Doreen:
I wish to trade places with you. I want all your powers, and you can have my dull, boring life.

Djinn:
Really? You mean it? That is, take my hand, O Great Mistress! *(They touch palm-to-palm)* As you have wished it, it shall be done! ABUL KELAH!!

They spin around as the blue and green fog swirl up. Doreen's headdress and alien skin are replaced with a vest and pantaloons. The Djinn dons Doreen's old sweatshirt and jeans. The fog begins to recede as the rummage sale table returns to right of center.

Doreen:
Rad!

Djinn:
These vestments are funky cool and comfy. No more shivering in that skimpy outfit for me!

Doreen:
I think I'll go to Hawai'i first, for a vacation.

Djinn:
You have to work some before you deserve a vacation.

Doreen:
Abul Kelah! *(Nothing happens.)* I'm still here. I feel... stuck.

Djinn:
You are now a Servant of the Lamp. You're only free to employ your powers in the service of one whom frees you from the prison between the worlds.

Doreen:
Prison! You never told me that! You tricked me!

Djinn:
People who don't listen often trick themselves.

Doreen:
I feel like I'm being sucked inside that lamp!

Djinn:
The spatial rift is opening and you are being called back home.

Doreen:
Help! Stop this! Change me back!

Djinn:
Sorry. Can't. Like, soooo *not* a Djinn anymore. See ya.
Doreen swirls offstage with the rest of the blue and green mist.

Sam walks up to the table.

Sam:
Oh, Doreen! There you are. I've been looking— Hey, you're not Doreen.

Djinn:
No, I'm not.

Sam:

Hi, I'm Sam. I was looking for my friend. She has a sweatshirt just like that.

Djinn:

I'm... I'm Jen. Yeah, she traded me something for it, and then she... took off.

Sam:

Just like her.

Djinn:

(Rummaging through the goods on the table with reverence) Many treasures can one find here....

Sam:

Oh, I love rummage sales, don't you?

Djinn:

I've never really... shopped at one. I wonder why people throw all their things away like this?

Sam:

They just get rid of stuff they have no use for, I guess. But a lot of this stuff is really cool. Like treasure. Doreen found this weird teapot —

Djinn:

You know, I'm starving. I feel like I haven't eaten in a thousand years.

Sam:

Me, too. Do you like Bongo Burger? It's just a few blocks from here, and today's free fries day!

Djinn:

Sometimes "free" can be pretty costly. I wonder if I have any money. *(Checking pockets)* Hey, I do!

Sam:

(Grabbing the Djinn's arm and pulling her offstage) And they use real barbecue sauce on their hamburgers. They're sooooo good. You'll love 'em!

They exit together, smiling and laughing.

BLACKOUT.

ALL THAT GLITTERS

Number of Characters: 4. Running Time: Under 20 Minutes.

The bumbling Behr Brothers thought they had struck gold when they kidnapped the heiress to the Golden Throne port-a-pottie empire... boy were they wrong! Gilda puts the Behrs through their paces, teaching them that all that glitters is NOT gold! Inspired by the classic tale "Golilocks," this play features lots of fast-paced dialogue, and is great for creating an old time radio-style audioplay!

Characters:

The Behr Brothers
Paul

Marion

Nigel

The Hostage
Gilda Goldstein

Setting: A small cabin in the middle of the Wild Woods.

The front door is situated in the corner stage right. It enters into the cabin's kitchen, which is decorated simply, in a clean country manner. Three chairs of differing styles surround a small table cloaked in gingham. Three settings of food sit untouched on the table.

Up stage left there is the exit to the hallway where the bedrooms are.

Up center the kitchen window, with blue gingham curtains, looks into the woods. Shadows from the trees outside make creepy designs against the gingham curtains.

Down stage left sits a blue sofa, bathed in shadow. On the sofa slumbers a curled up figure, covered by an afghan blanket.

The sound of feet tramping through the forest rise from offstage. The shadows of three figures pass by the window toward the front door of the cabin.

> Marion (Offstage):

Home again, home again, jiggety-jig!
> Paul (Offstage):

Oh, stop the singing and just up the door, you ninny!
> Marion (Offstage):

All righty, Paulie. Don't be so impatient.
> Paul (Offstage):

I'll show you how to be a patient in hospital if you don't let us in right quick!
> Marion (Offstage):

Ow!! That smarts!!! Give off!!

Sound of keys CLINKING in the lock of the door.

> Paul (Offstage):

Well? Open it, then?
> Marion (Offstage):

It's stuck. I can't get it open.
> Paul (Offstage):

It's *not* stuck.
> Marion (Offstage):

It *is* stuck, Paulie. You can plainly see —
> Paul (Offstage):

Oh, bother. Let me...

Sound of a scuffle outside the door. The door RATTLES violently.

> Nigel (Offstage):

I has to go to the baffroom.
> Marion (Offstage):

He has to go to the bathroom, Paulie.
> Paul (Offstage):

Stop yer gabbin' and let me work this, you ninny.
> Marion (Offstage):

Paulie, he *has to go to the bathroom*

Paul (Offstage):
Well, let him go, then! There's a whole bloody wood out here where a lad can relieve himself!

Marion (Offstage):
Paulie, you know that's not sanitary.

Paul (Offstage):
Shut it, I almost got it...

Marion (Offstage):
Here, let me help —

Paul (Offstage):
You're in me light... hey now!

Marion (Offstage):
Nigel wants to help, too.

Paul (Offstage):
The both of you move! My shoes! Nigel, I'm going to —

The front door is forced open with a crash. Three large burly men tumble through. Marion falls on top of Paul on the kitchen floor. These are the Three Behrs, a notorious band of Cockney Crooks.

PAUL, the oldest, is shorter than the other two, and very scruffy. An unlit cigar constantly sits in his mouth.

MARION sports a full beard and dresses like a lumberjack. He holds two large paper grocery sacks filled with goods. As he falls the groceries fall out onto the floor.

NIGEL, the youngest, is also the largest. He is very childlike.

Nigel walks through the door behind his brothers. Seeing them on the floor, he thinks they are playing a game, and leaps upon them, dog-pile style.

Marion:
Nigel, please!!

Paul:
Get that big ox off me!!!

Marion:
Nigel,
Paulie would like you to get off and let us up.

Nigel slowly rolls off his brothers and stands up. He lumbers toward the hallway and offstage.

Marion rises and starts picking up the groceries that have cascaded out of the bags and are now scattered across the room.

Paul lies on the floor in a contorted position.

Marion:

Paulie, get up. You look silly down there.
Paul:
I can't. I think me back is broke.
Marion:
Oh, come now. It is not. Help me put these groceries away.
Paul:
I can't, I tell you! That big ox crushed me spine!
Marion:
(Calling down the hallway) Nigel! Hurry up in there! You need to help Paul get up from the floor! He's thrown his back out again!
Paul:
Don't let that boy near me!

Marion busily picks up the scattered groceries and putting them away. As he moves about the cabin, he straightens things up a bit. A picture on the wall, the jars of dry goods on the counter and the like.

Marion:
We can't very well have you lying there in the middle of the room now can we? It's almost time for tea. *(Nigel enters.)* Nigel, please you're your big brother into a chair. Oh, but this room is dingy!
Marion crosses to the window in the living room and opens the curtains.

The figure on the couch is illuminated. Golden curly locks of hair poke from one end of the colorful afghan blanket.

Paul:
No! I'm feeling better!
Paul tries to raise himself from his position on the floor. His attempt is very painful and unsuccessful.

Nigel reaches down and slips his massive arms underneath Paul's shoulders. He lifts his brother easily to his feet, then carries him, rather like a rag doll, to the large wooden chair in the kitchen and plops him down into it.

Marion:
There. Now that you're in your hard chair your back should feel much better.
Paul:
(Wincing in pain and rubbing his lower back) Much better....

Nigel peeks at the figure on the couch.

Nigel:
Shhhh.... sleeping.

Marion:
Oh, I nearly forgot about her!

Paul:
How can you? She's the reason we're stuck out here in the middle of the woods. Nigel, check to see that she's secure.

Nigel gently lifts back the blanket, revealing a girl in a pretty yellow dress. Her hands and feet are tied up and a cloth has been tied over her mouth as a muffling gag. She appears to have slept through all the commotion.

Marion:
Perhaps we should wake her up for tea.

Marion goes into the kitchen and checks to see of there is water in the kettle. Turns a knob on the little stove.

Paul:
She gets nothing until we hear back from Goldstein.

Marion:
We can't let her starve.

Paul:
Starve?!? You saw how much she ate at breakfast! That "girl" put so much into her stomach that we had to go into town for more food and risk being seen in town. I'll not have her eating me out of house and home, thank you. What time is it?

Marion looks at a small clock in the kitchen.

Marion:
Four o'clock.

Paul:
Good. Goldstein is supposed to leave the money at our pre-arranged point-of-contact at four thirty.

Marion:
Do you think her father will really give us five million dollars for her safe return?

Paul:
He'd better, if he knows what's good for him. And her. Otherwise...

Paul draws his finger across his throat in the classic symbol of offing someone. He makes a sick sound, emulating the noise made when slitting someone's throat.

                Marion:
It would be such a shame to harm her. She's such a pretty thing.

                Nigel:
Pretty.

                Paul:
Come away from her, ox. Help Marion with the tea.
Marion retrieves bread and some sandwich spreads from the cupboard.

Nigel goes into the kitchen and pulls the dirty dishes off the table. He makes several trips from the table to the sink against the far wall, bumping the chair that Paul is in each time.

                Paul:
What are we having for tea? I'm famished.

Marion spreads the sandwiches, stacking them on a plate. As he does, Nigel takes a bite of each one, unnoticed by Marion.

                Marion:
Liverwurst sandwiches.
                Paul:
I hate liverwurst sandwiches!
                Marion:
The cold box is still on the fritz, I'm afraid.
                Paul:
Why didn't you buy devilled ham? I told you to buy the devilled ham.
                Marion:
It was too expensive. All we can afford is the liverwurst.
                Paul:
When we get the money from Goldstein we'll never have to eat liverwurst every again. We'll be able to have devilled ham every day, any time we want! With watercress, the way the royals have it for their tea.
                Marion:
Oh, that would be lovely.
                Nigel:
I likes liverwurst.
                Paul:
Of course you do.

GILDA, the girl on the sofa stirs. She sits up and stretches, confined by the restraints on her ankles and wrists. She acts as though she barely notices that she is tied up.

Gilda:
Mmmm...

Marion:
She's awake!

Paul:
Thank you for the advanced notice. Now see if she's all right.
Marion goes to Gilda and pulls down the cloth from around her mouth.

Gilda:
This bed was so comfy. I can't believe dozed off like that.

Paul:
It's a sofa and you've been asleep for at least three hours. I swear all you rich people do is sleep and eat.

Gilda:
What smells so good? I'm starving. What's for lunch?

Nigel brings a plate of the sandwiches toward the sofa.

Nigel:
We're haffin' liverwurst sandies.

Gilda:
My absolute favorite!

Nigel:
Mine, too.

Paul gets up and snatches the plate of sandwiches from Nigel just before he can offer it to Gilda.

Paul:
I said she gets nothing until we get word from her father.

Gilda:
My dad won't bend to your demands, you know. He'll call out the FBI and the National Guard to find me!

Paul:
Not if he wants his little golden girl back in once piece, miss. Now hush up.

Marion:

Paulie, I really think we ought to give her a little something to eat. She's a growing child.

Paul:
I won't have her taking good food like these sandwiches you slaved over – *(Paul looks at the plate of sandwiches in his hand. Each one has a bite mark out of it.)* NIGEL!!!

Marion:
Paulie, don't yell so! You know he's a growing boy, too.

Nigel:
I just tooks little bittle bites.

Paul holds the plate at arms length; turns his nose away from it.

Paul:
I can't eat these when they have his saliva all over them.
Marion takes the plate of sandwiches and puts them on the table.

Marion:
Are you sure?

Gilda:
I don't mind if Nigel's taken a nibble from them. He's sweet.

Marion:
Well, since Paul has decided to forego today's tea, I guess there's enough for you, Miss Goldstein.

Gilda:
Oh, goody!

Gilda holds her hands in front of her, as if showing them that she is still tied up.

Paul:
Not bloody likely.

Gilda:
How am I supposed to eat when my hands are tied up like this?

Paul:
Perhaps you'll eat less this time, then.

Marion:
Paulie, we needn't be inhumane to our guest.

Paul:
Guest! I like that! She's not a "guest," Marion. She's our hostage.

Marion:
Hostage or not, we still need to treat her in a civilized manner, Nigel.

Nigel sits on the couch and starts to untie her wrist bonds.

Nigel:

Pretty.

Paul:

Just make sure you leave the feet bound, ox.

Gilda:

(To Nigel) This is so kind of you.

Paul:

Don't get used to it.

Nigel helps Gilda to her feet and then to the kitchen table. She hops each step of the way. Nigel leads her to Paul's chair.

Gilda sits in it, but displays apparent discomfort.

He helps her to her feet again and leads her to Marion's plush chair. She nearly sinks into it. Nigel pulls her out of the chair and then, with a shy smile, offers his own diminutive stool. She sits down elegantly and looks up at him, smiling.

Gilda:

Perfect.

Paul sits on the sofa, exasperated.

Paul:

Is her majesty all settled, then?

Gilda daintily takes a bite of a sandwich.

Gilda:

Mmmm... scrumptious. You are such a good cook, Mr. Marion.

Marion:

Why thank you, my dear.

Gilda:

And I must say, I love what you've done with this place. It's so... quaint.

Marion:

The challenge, of course, is making a nice home on such limited resources.

Gilda:

It reminds me a little of a cabin my folks used to have at Lake Tahoe. Without the hot tub or cable TV. Of course.

Marion:

Oh, how lovely! A cabin at Lake Tahoe! I'm sure you must have enjoyed many a wonderful family moment there.

Gilda:

Actually, I usually would just go there with my friends. It was really rather a lonely place. I haven't been to it in years. I'm not even sure if we still own it.

Paul:

See how the rich are! They don't even know what they've got and what they haven't!

Gilda:

Well, perhaps you'll start forgetting things when you get my father's money. You know what they say: Money changes people.

Marion:

Oh, that would be tragic. Wouldn't it, Paulie?

Paul:

Oh, give off.

Marion:

I hadn't thought about that. I don't want to change, Paulie.

The teakettle emits a whistle. Marion bolts to the stove and turns off the knob. Retrieves a couple of teacups already prepared with tea bags from the cupboard and pours water into them.

Paul:

You most assuredly will not change, Marion. I, however, have many plans to change.

Marion carries the tea to the table and places a cup in front of Gilda.

Gilda:

Thank you. Did you know that my family came here back in the Great Depression? We weren't always wealthy. My great-grandfather cleaned toilets for forty years. My grandfather learned the trade, and that's how he got the idea to open a company that rents commodes to construction sites and fairs. Now we supply Porty-Toidies to five different states. Daddy calls them the "Golden Thrones."

Paul:

So you're saying that your family is full of —

Marion:

(Interrupting) Your family is very corrupt because of all the money they have?

Gilda:

I don't know about corrupt, but we aren't the closest of families. I mean, not like you and your brothers. You seem very close with one another.

Marion:
Oh, we are. We're quite devoted to one another.

Paul:
May we change the subject, please?

Marion:
Do you think money will really change us?

Gilda:
I would hate to see that devotion to each other be destroyed.

Marion:
How would that happen?

Gilda:
Well, the first thing to go is living on a budget. I mean, you got a deal on this delicious liverwurst, right?

Marion:
Oh, yes. It was three for sixty-nine cents. A very good bargain, if I must say!

Gilda:
You won't care about the cost of your liverwurst after you become rich. You'll end up paying any amount just to have it. And then, when all the money has been spent on liverwurst, you'll need more and more money, because you'll have become used to spending money on the expensive stuff.

Nigel:
What about tuna?

Gilda:
I've known people — friends of my parents — who would spend as much as five dollars for a can of tuna.

Marion:
No!

Gilda:
Yes!

Marion:
My word.... Five dollars a tin!

Nigel begins to blubber.

Paul:
Enough of this ridiculousness. She's just trying to confuse you. I don't mind telling you that I for one will not mind paying as much as five dollars for a tin of my favourite devilled ham.

Gilda:
I hope you weren't making plans to spend the entire five million, when really you'll get much less.

Marion:
Much less?

Paul:

I demanded five million.

Gilda:
You are going to split it three ways, aren't you?

Paul:
Naturally. We're brothers.

Gilda:
I just did the math. Roughly, each of you will get one-point-six million dollars out of the five million that my Daddy will pay you for my safe return. It's much easier to go through one-point-six million than it is five million.

Marion:
One-point-six *is* much less than five million, you're right.

Paul:
Don't listen to her, Marion. It's plenty for each of us. We'll be able to have everything we've ever wanted.

Gilda:
You'll spend it until it's all gone and then you'll want more. And then where will you be?

Marion:
It sounds like some sort of sickness to me.

Gilda:
(Whispering conspiratorially to Marion) It's called "Gold Fever." People become greedy and paranoid.

Nigel:
(Conspiratorially) I had the measles once.

Paul:
What's all that whispering going on over there?

Gilda:
(Whispering) You see? And he doesn't even have the money yet.

Marion:
Paulie, you aren't going to want all the devilled ham for yourself, are you? Not at five dollars a tin!

Paul:
That's it! *(Bolting up from the sofa and suddenly remembering his hurt back)* Ow! Enough of her worrisome blathering. Nigel, put the gag back on her.

Nigel:
But then she won't be able to talk.

Paul:
Precisely. Marion, clean up the tea.

Gilda:
I see Marion cooking and cleaning up around here. And Nigel doing everything you tell him to do. What else do you do besides give all the orders, Mr. Behr?

Paul:
I, my witty girl, give the orders because I am Eldest, and the brains of this outfit. And when I have to, I take matters into my own hands.

Paul crosses to the table and pulls the cloth around Gilda's mouth. He walks away.

When his back is turned, Gilda pulls the gag down herself.

Gilda:
I'm not done eating.

Paul:
Tie her up again!!!

Gilda:
My father won't like it at all when he's learned that you've been unkind to me.

Marion:
Oh, we haven't been unkind, have we??

Gilda:
Well, not you, Mr. Marion. And certainly not sweet Nigel, here. But Mr. Paul has, with his shouting and his ordering. Perhaps when I talk to my father, I'll tell him to give you and Nigel your share, and leave Mr. Paul's share out of the ransom.

Paul:
You can't do that!

Marion:
Could you?

Paul:
He's going to leave the money under the bridge behind a boulder marked with special graffiti. She won't be able to tell him anything.

Gilda:
I must say that these were the most delectable liverwurst sandwiches I've ever eaten. Thank you so much.

Paul:
What time is it?!?

Nigel looks at the clock.

Nigel:
The big hand is on the six.

Paul:
Big hand on... it's four thirty!

Nigel:
...and the little bittle hand is on –

Paul:
Time to go to the bridge. Marion, you watch her closely. Nigel, you stay away from her.

Gilda:
What time will you be back?

Paul:

What concern is that of yours?
>					Gilda:
I just want to know if you actually will be back, or if you plan to take all the money for yourself and go to Switzerland.
>					Paul:
Switzerland! Wherever did you get that idea?
>					Marion:
Switzerland! Oh, Paulie, you wouldn't go to Switzerland and leave us here, would you?
>					Paul:
No one is going to Switzerland!
>					Gilda:
I know a lovely hotel in Lausanne on Lake Geneva. You know, I could contact them and tell them to treat you as special guests. Mr. Paul, you really should take your brothers to Switzerland. It's lovely this time of year.
>					Paul:
No Switzerland!
>					Marion:
But I've always dreamed of going to Switzerland.
>					Paul:
You have not.
>					Nigel:
I wants to go on holiday.
>					Gilda:
Of course, it all depends on whether Mr. Paul does come back with the money...
>					Marion:
You are going to return with all the money, won't you, Paulie?
>					Paul:
Of course, Marion. We are brothers, aren't we?
>					Gilda:
Shouldn't one of you go with him just to make sure?
>					Nigel:
I'm sure we're brothers.
>					Paul:
Look, Marion, the two of you need to stay to guard our golden girl here. I shall go to the boulder under the bridge, retrieve the parcel containing all of our fabulous money therein, and return, post-haste. Then we shall release this annoying little girl so that she can go back to her toilet-scrubbing father and not fill your head with any more ridiculous notions. Is that all clear?
>					Marion:
Nigel, I want you to go with Paulie and make sure he comes back with the money.
>					Paul:
Marion! Be reasonable!

Marion:
You've got the Gold Fever, Paulie. It's effected your judgment. We can't take a chance that you'll run off with all of it. Then Nigel and I would be stuck here with nothing. We promised Mother we'd take care of each other.

Paul:
And we have. We will! It's getting late. I have to go to the rendezvous.

Gilda:
Don't bother.

Marion:
Why not?

Gilda:
If I'm right, the money's not going to be there.

Paul:
What are you saying?

Suddenly spotlights beam through the woods outside the window of the cabin.

Cop *(Offstage)*:
All right, Behrs! We have you surrounded! Release Gilda Goldstein and come out with your hands up!

Paulie:
Coppers! How did they--?

Gilda:
I ate all of that food this morning on purpose, knowing that you would have to go to the market to get more. And let me tell you, that with my girlish figure, that was hard to do. All those bangers! Let's just say you're lucky you weren't here for the next couple of hours. Anyway, I figured someone would spot you and follow you back here to your secret hideout.

Paul:
And you kept talking to Marion –

Gilda:
...because I wanted to keep you here until the police came.

Cop *(Offstage)*:
You have one minute to send out the Goldstein girl, Behrs!

Marion:
And I thought she was sweet. Oh, Paulie, what will we do?

Paul:
Surrender, Marion. It's all we can do now.

Nigel begins to eat the rest of the liverwurst sandwiches greedily.

Marion:

Nigel! Don't be such a hoggity-all!

Paul:

Oh, let him. It's probably the last time in a very long time that he'll have his liverwurst sandies.

Marion:

At least we'll be together, just like Mother wanted.

Paul:

Oh, joy of joys...

Gilda bends down and unties her ankle restraints. She walks spryly to the front door, opens it, then turns back to the Behr Brothers before striding over the threshold.

Gilda:

A little something for you to remember: All that glitters is not gold.

She exits gaily.

The Three Behrs hold their hands up and file out of the cabin, sulking, toward the spotlights.

BLACKOUT.

CANDY IS DANDY

Number of Characters: 3 Running Time: About 15 minutes

Inspired by the classic "Hansel and Gretal," this dark tale tells the story of a brother and sister who meet a woman named Candy. Is she really as nice as she seems? Who's really the villain here?

Characters:

Greta

Hal

Candace

Setting: **The Wild Woods**

Trees upstage, bushes downstage. The light is gold, as the sun sets.

A large motor home engine revs offstage. By the sound we can tell it pulls away.

A breathless girl, age 11, bursts through the brush from far right upstage. This is GRETA. She wears shorts and tee-shirt, bandana on her head, colorful knapsack on her back. She is very out of place in the woods. She seems scared and a bit in shock.

Greta:

No!!

The sound of leaves rustling come from where Greta entered. A small boy, age 8, climbs through the brush to enter on stage with difficulty. This is HAL, Greta's little brother. He carries a stick as if it were a weapon. He hacks at the branches of the foliage, doing battle with them.

Hal:

Hai-yah! Yah!!

Greta:

Quiet, Hal!

Greta walks around the stage a bit, scoping out the situation.

Hal:

Greta, where's Mom and Dad?

Greta:

I knew we should have hurried more. They're gone!

Hal:

Gone?

Greta:

Yeah, gone! Do you see the motor home anywhere around here?

Hal:

I don't see it.

Greta:

That's 'cause it's gone. You and your stupid stick you just had to have...

Hal:

I needed a sword. To fight the monsters in the woods and protect us.

Greta:

We spent so much time looking for the perfect one that Dad and Mom left us!

Hal:

They couldn't've.

Greta:

They did!

Hal:

They probably just went to get gas or something. Or lunch. I'm hungry.

Greta:

I told Mom I needed a cell phone for my birthday!

Hal:

We could call Batman!

Greta:

Yeah, or Dad on his cell and tell him he left us behind. *(Turning to Hal and crossing to him, she holds his shoulders protectively.)* Don't be scared, Hal. I'm going to get us out of this. Everything's going to be okay!

Hal:

Get us out of what?

Greta:

Out of these woods. Away from the dangers.

Hal:

I like it here. *(With great bravado he brandishes his "sword" with a flourish.)* I laugh at danger! Ha ha! I am Hal the Mighty! No dragon can defeat me! Hai yah! Yah! Yah!

Greta grabs him and pulls him down to a crouching position.

Greta:

Stop it! You'll let all the animals know we're here! We've got to be real quiet...

Hal:

I want to live in the jungle and grow up like Tarzan.

Greta:

This isn't the jungle. It's the woods. The Wild Woods. With bears and skunks and puma...

Hal:

And wolves! *(Growling and scraping like a wolf.)* Grrrrrrr..... We can be part of the wolf family like Mowgli. Grrrrrrrr...... And then Baloo the Bear could teach me how to eat ants.

Greta:

Hal, wolves are not nice and would not invite us home for dinner... unless we were going to be their dinner. Wolves eat people. Bears eat people.

Hal:

They do not. Wolves only eat other animals when they are really hungry. And bears fish like Dad and his buddies.

Greta:

You're so stupid! I can't believe they left us like that! We're so screwed! I hate it here! I didn't wanna go on a stupid family vacation in a stupid Tioga to the stupid Wild Woods anyway! I'm cold and I'm hungry and I wanna go home!!! *(Hal walks away from his sister and starts to sulk. Greta turns to notice him.)* What???

Hal:

Stupid is not a nice word. We don't say stupid. I'm not stupid.

Greta:

I'm sorry, Hally. You're not stupid. It's just this whole thing is stupid. Dad and Mom are stupid for leaving us here.

Hal:

(Screaming) Mom and Dad are not stupid!!!

Greta:

(Matching his volume) Yes they are!!!

Hal:

Are not! Are not! Are not!

Greta:

Shut up! The bears will hear you!

Hal:

I don't care! Mom and Dad are not stupid! Take it back!!!

Greta:

(Quieting down) All right, all right... I take it back. Dad and Mom are not stupid. Now come on, be quiet for a sec. I gotta figure this whole thing out.

Hal:

The wolves will teach us how to hunt for rabbits and the bears will teach us where all the good dessert stuff is. Like honey with berries and we could make jam and ---

Greta:

Shhh! Maybe would could follow the tire tracks to the main road and wait for a cop to find us there.

The lights dim a bit and turn to cooler tones as night begins to fall in the Wild Woods.

Hal:

That's a good idea, Greta.

Greta starts looking all over the ground for the tire tracks from the motor home.

Greta:

It's getting too dark! I can't see 'em! Oh, we'll never get out of here!

Hal:

We can follow them in the morning.

Greta:

In the morning we'll be bear food. *(A rustling in the bushes comes from the far left corner upstage.)* What's that?? Omigawd, it's a bear! I just know it!

Hal runs to Greta and holds on to her.

Through the brush upstage enters a woman of some advanced years. CANDACE appears to be about 70, but in excellent condition, spry like a doe. She's dressed as if she's at home in the woods, much like a scout: khaki safari shirt and shorts; kerchief around her neck; hiking boots; strong walking stick; large wacky hat on her head.

Candace:

Well, hello there, dears. Wherever did you two come from?

Hal:

We're from Ottawa.

Greta:

Hal, shhhh!

Candace:

Ottawa is a beautiful city! The Parliament Building there is like a palace. And what brings you here to the Wild Woods?

Hal:

We're on vacation.

Greta:

We *were* on vacation. But we sort of got... lost here.

Hal:

Mom and Dad drove away and left us.

Candace:

Oh, dear. That sounds serious.

Hal:

We're going to be raised by wolves now.

Candace:

The wolves around here are very nice, but I'm not sure they could raise a pair of human children.

Greta:

Are you camping here?

Candace:

Goodness, no. I live in the Wild Woods.

Greta:

You live here?

Candace:

Yes, dear. My cabin is just through those trees over there.

Candace points to the far right entrance through which Greta and Hal had come.

Greta:

I didn't see any house over there.

Candace:

Come, I'll show you. I can't imagine how you could have missed it.

Candace leads the children across the stage. As she does so, the trees upstage part. Candace's cabin moves forward, finally taking its position down stage right.

The cabin is cottage-style and has been brightly painted. Each panel seems to be a different hue. Flowers and other whimsical designs have been painted all over the small facade. A large comical happy face adorns the front door of the cabin.

Hal:

Wow! Your house is cool!

Greta:

Do you have a phone?

Candace:

No, dear, I don't keep a telephone. The civic power lines do not extend this far into the Wild Woods, I'm afraid. I'm what you might call "off the grid." Even my electricity comes from a gasoline generator.

Hal:

Does that mean you don't have cable?

Candace:

That would be a correct deduction, young man.

Greta:

Gasoline! You must have a car!

Candace:

I'm sorry, no. My only mode of transportation are the legs God gave me. I haven't driven a vehicle in years.

Greta:

Then how do you go to the store and buy stuff?

Candace:

Why, I have very little need of anything at the markets in town, my dear. The woods provide sustenance enough to keep me healthful. I make my own clothes....

Hal:

What about candy?

Candace:

You know, that's funny you should ask, young man. I've been so rude, I haven't told you my name. I'm Candace. My friends call me Candy. Would you call me Candy?

Greta:

You have friends?

Candace:

And what are your names, dear?

Greta:

I'm Greta, and this is my brother Hal.

Candace:

It certainly is a pleasure to make both of your acquaintances.

They shake hands.

Hal:

Hi, Candy!

Candace:

My, but your hands are so boney, young man! Come inside for dinner. We'll fatten you up.

Greta:

I don't know if we should....

Hal:

Greta, I'm hungry!

Candace:

Don't be silly, my dear. I have a nice stew that's been simmering all day. I would love to serve the two of you tonight.

Greta:

Well, I'm hungry, too.

Candace opens the door to the cabin. The front of the cabin spins around to become the inside of the cabin. Trees spin around to become the fireplace and the cauldron containing the stew. A bush down stage spins around to reveal a work table.

Candace:

Welcome to my humble abode.

Hal:

Mmmm... smells good. I'm starving.

Candace:

You certainly look like you could use a good meal, young man. Now make yourself at home while your sister and I set the table for dinner.

Candace leads Greta to a cupboard from where she retrieves cutlery and dishes. She loads up Greta's arms with the place settings. Hal explores the cabin.

Greta:

Where's the dining table?

Candace:

Right there, my dear.

Greta:

It looks like a work bench.

Greta starts to set the table, very much not amused. Candace proceeds to scoop out stew from the kettle into large ceramic bowls. She carries them to the table, one by one.

Candace:

Very astute! It's a wonderful surface. I do all my work here.

Hal:

What do you do?

Candace:

I'm an artist. I take objects from the woods to create my pieces. Why, just this morning I finished that piece there.

She points to a skull on the wall that has been adorned with acorns and other natural items.

Hal:

Cool!

Greta:

You mean *that* was on here?

Candace:

Yes, dear.

Hal:

Did you kill it?

Candace:

Not that one. I found the poor animal near the interstate. Someone had hit it with their vehicle. Now, who's hungry?

Hal comes running to the table.

Greta:

I've lost my appetite.

Candace:

More for us, then! Dig in, Hal.

Hal and Candace eat voraciously, making sounds of joy and satisfaction.

Hal:

This is so good!

Candace:

Eat up, Hal, eat up! We need to get you plump. Greta, if you are not going to eat, would you be a dear and you make yourself useful by stoking the oven? After dinner I shall make a date-nut cake with brambleberry dressing for dessert. How does that sound?

Hal:

What's brambleberry?

Candace:

It's simply one of the most delicious of all the woodland berries! The bramble bushes are full of them, but they have these sharp little thorns that will cut you up to ribbons if you are not careful! See, these wounds are from my last battle with the brambles.

Candace pulls up her sleeve and shows Hal red marks on her arm.

Hal:

Cool! *(Showing her a bandage on his knee.)* I got this when I slid down some rocks into the creek.

Candace:

What was in the creek?

Hal:

A big alligator!

Candace:

How exciting!

Greta:

It was a tadpole.

Hal:

We were gonna fight!

Candace:

Very brave!

Greta:

I told you not to go down there, 'cause you'd slip if you did. And you did!

Candace:

Come, come. To little eyes, a tadpole could well seem an alligator.

Hal:

Wanna see?

Candace:

Indeed!

Hal pulls off the bandage to reveal a nasty scab. Candace squeals with delight.

Hal:

Gross, huh!

Candace:

Delicious! Now, I think it's time to stoke the oven. *(Crossing to the fireplace.)* Greta, if you'll help me....

Greta:

If I have to....

Candace:

Only if you want dessert! What you need to do place the small sticks on the bottom, then the larger pieces on top of them. Cherry wood is what I prefer, though walnut and pine can add an interesting aspect to the flavour, too.

Candace hands sticks from a woodpile next to the oven to Greta. Greta slowly, reluctantly, places the wood into the oven.

Greta:

Ow!

Candace:

Be careful! It's still hot from the stew. But we need to get it even hotter for baking!

Hal:

I am soooo full....

Candace:

Oh, my brave little boy. You've had such a daring day. Why don't you take a little nap while we bake.

She leads him over to a large seat in which he curls up and falls asleep.

Greta:

So, you live alone here in this cabin....

Candace:

For fifteen years now.

Greta:

Why?

Candace:

I beg your pardon.

Greta:

Why do you live alone? Don't you have family?

Candace:

Everyone has family, dear.... but not everyone wants to live near family.

Greta:

Do you have children?

Candace:

My husband and I had a whole parcel of little ones! But they grew up a long time ago, and moved away. Most of them live in the City.

Greta:

Why don't you live there?

Candace:

Family is important, but so is being free. I could never be free in the City, child. I am an artist and the Wild Wood is my palette!

Greta:

Do you ever see them? Your family?

Candace:

Not in many years....

Greta:

Don't you get lonely? Don't you miss your kids?

Candace:

It was good to be a mother, but in the end, they had to go.

Greta:

Maybe that's what Mom and Dad thought, too. We had to go....

Hal wakes up and rubs his eyes.

Hal:

Where are we going?

Greta:

I don't know....

Hal runs to Candace and embraces her.

Hal:

We can stay here, right?

Greta:

Hal, we can't stay here. We have to get home.

Candace:

You can stay here until we find a way to contact your parents.

Hal:

That would be so cool!

Greta:

What if Mom and Dad don't want us anymore?

Candace:

In that event, we'd have to find some other use for you! How is the oven coming, dear?

Greta:

It's very hot.

Candace pats Hal's tummy.

Candace:

Looks like you've had almost to eat, young man.

Greta:

Can you show us how to get out of the woods and back to the main road?

Candace:

Certainly.

Greta:

So we can go in the morning?

Candace:

In a few days. I am in the middle of several projects at present... and you can help me with them! It will be nice to have an extra pair of hands helping clear up all the clutter I make. I swear, I spend most of my time cleaning up!

Hal:

I want to help!

Greta:

I don't want to stay here! I want to go home. We have to find Mom and Dad.

Candace:

As soon as they realize you are gone, I am certain they will come back to the Wild Woods to look for you. So the sensible thing to do is stay here in my cabin, instead of gallivanting all over creation in search of your parents. In a few days when my project is complete, I will escort you to the nearest ranger station where Mike the Ranger will be able to assist in your family reunion. Now, who's up for making a cake?

Candace begins to gather ingredients and put them on the work table. Greta backs away.

Greta:

No phone. No car. No one even knows we're here. *(She grabs Hal and pulls him into a corner so they can talk privately.)* Listen, Hally. This is important. We have to get out of here. I don't trust this old lady.

Hal:

She's nice.

Greta:

She's not nice. She's not going to take us to find Mom and Dad.

Hall:

She's making us a cake.

Greta:

Yeah, of what? Dead squirrel? Yuck.

Candace:

(Calling over) Greta, would you be so kind as to hand me the big roasting pot on the shelf?

Greta:

For the cake?

Candace:

Oh, it's going to rise.

Greta:

Look, Hal... we're getting out of here. I don't think she's planning to make a cake. The way she keeps looking at you, and pinching you... Hal, I think she's going to cook you up and eat you!

Hal starts to bawl. Greta clamps her hand over his mouth.

Don't you start that, Hally. Not right now. We've got to find a way out of here before she kills you and turns you into one of her art pieces.

Candace:

Greta, the roasting pot. I need it now.

Greta gives Hal a look. She puts her free hand to her mouth, making the "Sssh" sign with her finger pressed to her lips. Hal nods, agreeing that he will not cry out.

Greta releases Hal, then crosses to the shelf where a large roasting pot hangs. She pulls it down, and stealthily steps to Candace, who is busy mixing her ingredients.

Greta:

I have it, Candace.

Hal:

Candy!!!

Candace:

That's right. Candy, dear. Call me "Candy!"

Greta swings and hits Candace in the back of the head with the roasting pot. Candace makes a sickening cry and falls to the floor.

Hal screams, then cries. Greta stares at Candace's body for a few seconds, then drops the roasting pot. She runs back to Hal and tries to calm him.

Greta:

It's okay, it's okay, Hal. She's okay. She's gonna be okay. She just had to go to sleep so we could leave and find Mom and Dad. She's okay. It's all okay.

Hal:

She's bleeding.

Greta:

She's not bleeding.

Hal:

From her head. She's bleeding. That's so gross!

Greta pulls Hal to his feet. She starts to drag him to the door.

Greta:

We have to go now, Hally. We have to find that ranger station. Come on. Where's my Hal the Mighty, hunh? Only Hal the Mighty can get us out of this. Come on, Hal. Are you going to be my Hal the Mighty?

Hal:

(Wiping his eyes) I guess so....

Greta takes a look around the cabin, and STEALS SOMETHING – What does she steal? She and Hal begin to exit.

The lights dim to cast shadows throughout the cabin.

Candace slowly rises from the ground. She reached out her arms in the direction of the voice of her son Mike.

Candace

Brains...brains! Must...have...<u>brains</u>!

Greta and Hall run out of the cabin, screaming!

Candace (*Laughing*)

Ha ha ha! Gets them every time!

BLACKOUT!

Select Scenes from

CINDY CLAUS VERSUS THE EASTER BUNNY

Number of Characters: 5. Running Time: About 15 minutes.

"Cindy Claus Versus the Easter Bunny" is the sequel to "Cindy Claus Saves Christmas." Former villain Anti-Claus, Santa's evil twin brother, is bored! So hatches a plan to take control over all the chocolate in the world!

Characters

Anti-Claus, Santa Claus' twin brother
E.B. the Easter Bunny, formerly known as Pete R. Cottentail
Cindy Claus, Santa's niece, and the heiress to the North Pole
Max, Anti-Claus' very tall elfen assistant.
Hershey, CEO of a chocolate company

ACT I: Scene One

Setting: The dressing Room of Widow Twankey in a London theatre.

Anti-Claus is discovered, sitting in front of his make-up table and mirror. Max (Shorty) fusses with the wardrobe.

Anti-Claus sighs long and loudly.

Max:

Why the sigh, Boss?

Anti-Claus:

Oh, nothing... nothing...

Max:

You've been so melancholy the past few days. Do you want to talk about it?

Anti-Claus:

There's nothing to talk about, really, it's just that I...

Max:

Don't you like being the Widow Twankey, Boss?

Anti-Claus:

Oh, of course I do. I've been given everything I've ever dreamed of: Fame, the adoration of children everywhere... I'm truly one of the symbols of Christmas now. It's just that I'm so... so bored.

Max:

It's a far cry from being the evil villain who tried to destroy Christmas every year, eh?

Anti-Claus:

That's just it. I don't 'try' for anything these days. There's no challenge! No scheming to get back at my twin brother, Santa. Nothing to cut my teeth on. I don't even have the desire to strike at Christmas, now that I'm part of the system.

Max:

Funny how it works that way, isn't it?

Knock on the door. Max crosses to it.

Max:

Who is it?

Delivery Boy: *(From outside of door)*

Delivery for the Widow Twankey!

Max opens the door. The Delivery Boy holds a box of chocolates. Max takes the box, gives the boy a small tip, and closes the door.

Max gives the chocolates to Anti-Claus.

Anti-Claus:

Chocolates! How lovely! *(Anti immediately opens the box and starts sampling the candy without offering any to Max.)*

Max:

There's a card.

Anti-Claus:

A card? Oh, it's from the Duke of Willoughsby. He says that his children adore me and he wanted to send his appreciation. I say, he must have seen my performance 15 times this season!

Max:

Funny, I've never seen his children in the audience.

Anti-Claus:

He certainly does know his way to a Widow's heart. I love chocolate. People don't realize it, but chocolate is one of the most important substances on Earth. I'm surprised that it's not as dear as gold.

Max:

Good thing, too. I don't think I could afford even one chocolate easter bunny if it were.

Anti-Claus:

You and your chocolate easter bunnies. I say, I've never seen anyone eat so many in a row as you.

Max:

I have. At least.

Anti-Claus: *(laughing lightly to self)*

You know, if one controlled all the chocolate in the world, one would control Easter.

Max:

Sure would put a crimp in the Easter Bunny's style.

Anti-Claus:

Yes, it would, wouldn't it...

Anti looks off in the distance while Max looks directly at him,

Max:

Now, Boss....

Anti-Claus:

You just gotta help me, Max. You just gotta! I've been so filled with ennui lately, and the answer to my problems has been staring me in the face all this time. I need to scheme, to plot, to plan. I need something to cut my teeth on. Something to give me a reason to get up in the morning. I can't get away from it: I gotta be me!

Max:

Oh, no, here we go again...

Anti-Claus:

That's right! Dust off the remote-controlled Snowbots and fire up the invisible sledge! We're taking over—EASTER!

Blackout.

ACT I: Scene Two

Setting: A room in the Easter Bunny's warren.

The Easter Bunny sits in a large chair, smoking a cigar, while Cindy Claus stands with a presentations board and pointer. Two elves accompany her.

Cindy Claus:

And so you see, Mister Bunny, that with our fleet of flying reindeer, Santa Claus Enterprises International is really your foremost option for the fulfillment of your Easter candy. Why, you could increase the distribution of your baskets by 15% this first season alone.

Easter Bunny:

Impressive. Well, that was a very thorough presentation, Ms. Claus. You people really have your stuff together up there in the tundra, don't you?

Cindy Claus:

(Smiling) Being in charge of the largest-scale holiday on the planet has forced us to be competitive, Mister Bunny. As you can see *(an elf flips to another chart)* here, while Christmas is celebrated on every continent, in every country, regardless of governmental religious restrictions, Easter holds only 65% of the market share for its season. We're rather proud of the work we do, and we'd like to use our skills and resources to help the other holiday organizations achieve the success that we've been able to accomplish. We're in the business of helping people, and we'd like to help you, sir.

Easter Bunny:

Oh, really? Well, you sure have helped me, wearing that cute little red miniskirt. Do you dress like that for all of your business meetings, or am I just 'special?'

Cindy Claus:

I'm not sure what you mean, Mister Bunny. We consider all of our prospective clients 'special.'

Easter Bunny:

Oh, so that's how he gets his many 'accounts.' Sending a hot little snow bunny like you to do his dirty work. *(Patting lap)* Why don't you come here and give me the rest of your 'presentation?'

Cindy Claus:

Mister Bunny!

Easter Bunny:

You know, you Clauses really have it all. You've got the huge Toyshop, and the castle, the elfin workforce, the flying reindeer... and you take 12 days to deliver all of your goods.

Cindy Claus:

That's correct, sir, and we —

Easter Bunny:

I don't have any of that. I'm just a working stiff, Ms. Claus. I built this organization from the ground up. It's just me and a very small group of egg-painters. I order all the chocolate, do all the books, and deliver every basket... myself. In one morning. Two, tops.

Cindy Claus:

And I'm sure that must be tiring—

Easter Bunny:

I don't get tired, Claus. I've got this one talent that allows me to do what I do, and forking over the 'fulfillment' of my operation to a bunch of antler-headed corsairs isn't going to help me any. It'd make me lazy.

Cindy Claus:

But don't you want to relax? To—

Easter Bunny:

Want an egg roll?

Cindy Claus:

Excuse me?

Easter Bunny:

(Pulling out hidden egg roll) Mmmm... got these at a little alleyway spring roll stand in Beijing.

Cindy Claus:

When did you get that?

Easter Bunny:

Just now. Between 'want an' and 'egg roll' I zipped over to China for some lunch. Fortune cookie? *(pulls out a small bag of fortune cookies, leisurely pulls one out and breaks it open)*

Cindy Claus:

How? I never saw you leave...

Easter Bunny:

Haven't you ever wondered how the Easter Bunny can deliver all of his baskets and hide all of the eggs in one morning, without the benefit of a huge workforce?

Cindy Claus:

Well, I—

Easter Bunny:

Speed.

Cindy Claus:

Speed?

Easter Bunny:

Speed. Ya see these? These are the fleetest feet ever to get a corn under God's green Earth.

Cindy Claus:

My goodness!

Easter Bunny:

You sure can bet your sweet goodness! I'm the fastest thing since Hermes stole the cows from Apollo. *(reading fortune –improvise it!)*
"_____."

Cindy Claus:

That's absolutely amazing, Mister Bunny.

Easter Bunny:

I do it all, toots. While you and that ho-ho-hoing tub of lard up there are sitting on your aurora borealis, telling your workers what to do, I'm down here racing all over kingdom come getting the job done. I've worked too long and too hard in this business to see it taken away by a mega-operation like yours.

Cindy Claus:

But we never—

Easter Bunny:

I know a take-over when I see one! I know what a 'third-party development' *really* is. Another word for 'buy-out.' Well this bunny ain't sellin'.

Cindy Claus:

Thank you very much for your time, Mister Bunny. I can see that this meeting is now over. Good day.

Easter Bunny:

Now you don't have to go away mad. We're both the types who like people to be happy. How 'bout you come back to my private chambers and let me make you 'happy?'

Cindy Claus:

Lay one paw on me, Mister Bunny and you will be lucky if it doesn't wind up dyed orange and attached to a key chain. My aunt warned me about you.

Easter Bunny:

Ah, yes, Mary Claus. What a skirt she was! Them legs!

Cindy Claus:

That is enough, Mister Bunny! I will not hear you speak this way. Aster, Schlomo, let's go.

They exit.

Easter Bunny:

Heh heh heh E.B., you still got it, you old hare. She'll come around. They always do.

Blackout.

ACT I: Scene Four

Setting: A Chocolate factory in Hershey Park, Pennsylvania.

Anti-Claus and Max in a meeting with the head of Hershey's corporation.

Anti-Claus:

It's so good doing business with you, Mr. Hershey. I look forward to seeing you on my quarterly tours of the factory.

Hershey:

Are you kiddin'? With the money I made off this deal, I'm not gonna stick around to manage the plant. I can retire for life! *(closes briefcase filled with money, dons hat)* It's Fiji or bust! *(Starts to exit, looks back.)* I never even liked chocolate! *(Exit)*

Anti-Claus:

Not like chocolate? He must be mad. Oh, well, what's next on the list, Max?

Max:

We've got Nestlé, Godiva, Whitman's, Schrafft's...

Anti-Claus:

Who's next on the list?

Max:

See's Candies out on the west coast.

Anti-Claus:

That upstart old woman.... How much money do we have left?

Max:

(Using calculator) 25.67 million.

Anti-Claus:

It will take every pound note that I made as the Widow Twankey, but I'm going to do it. By noon tomorrow, I will own every piece of chocolate in the world! *(Laughs maniacally)* My, I haven't laughed like that in months. It felt wonderful!

Blackout.

BIRDBRAINS

The BIRDBRAINS mini-episodes are sitcom-style sketches. The situation comedy for television is written in a specific format, but formatted for this digital edition. These sketches focus on the dialogue between the characters, and have limited stage direction – to leave it up to the imagination of the director! So go ahead and use a video recorder or three for these sketches. Use close-ups! Different angles! Have fun editing in post!

Sitcom/Movie Terms used in these scripts:

INT. Interior, indicating the inside of a building.

EXT. Exterior, used to indicate someplace outdoors.

V.O. Voice Over, an unseen voice.

SFX. Sound Effects

FADE IN. At the beginning of a scene, coming out of blackness on camera.

FADE OUT. At the end of a scene, going into blackness on camera.

Birdbrains

Episode 1: "Field Trip"

Number of characters: 5   Running Time: About ten minutes.

Characters

SYDNEY
The whiz-kid. A braniac with an encyclopedic mind. Affectionately called The Brain.

BIRD
Goofy, sees the world a little different than everyone else Sydney's best friend.

ALEX
Very wealthy. Has been everywhere and done everything.

BRETT
The panicky kid who worries about everything. A hypochondriac.

SASHA
A foreign exchange student.

FADE IN:
INT: THE MUSEUM OF NATURAL HISTORY

                    V.O.
...and please be sure to keep with your tour group
          at all times...

Enter ALEX, BRETT, SYDNEY, SASHA, and BIRD, five
school kids on a field trip.

                    BRETT
Are you sure this was the right way to go? I think
          we're lost. I don't see anyone.

                    BIRD
I see someone!

                    SYDNEY
Who?

                    BIRD
Him!

BIRD CROSSES TO A SARCOPHAGUS WITH A MUMMY IN IT.

                    SYDNEY
He doesn't count as a "someone." He's dead. It's
          an Egyptian mummy.

                    SASHA
In my country, we wrap our dead in silk and wax.

                    ALEX
Ew! What a waste of fine silk!

                    BRETT
Dead?!? You see dead people?

BIRD
I see dead people!

SYDNEY CROSSES TO THE SARCOPHAGUS AND INSPECTS THE PICTOGRAMS CLOSELY.

SYDNEY
And he's not a him, anyway. He's a she...I mean...It's the Princess Ananka, if I remember my hieroglyphics correctly...

BIRD
A princess?? I think I'm in love...

ALEX
This has to be the right way to go! I always know where I'm going. The lady at the information counter said to take a right, then a left, then another right and we'd find the room with all the dinosaurs in it.

SYDNEY
I thought she said left, right, left.

ALEX
Really?

BRETT
Oh, god, we're lost! Lost!

ALEX
We are not lost. Alex Van Chrysler does not get lost.

BRETT
We're lost, and I'm never going to see my mom again. What if my asthma acts up? Who's going to take me to the hospital? None of you can drive yet!

SYDNEY
Brett, you don't have asthma.

BRETT
I could start! Oh, I wish I had never left my lunch on the bus. And I had a meat loaf sandwich in my lunch today, too!

BIRD
I have an idea. Why don't we split up? Alex can take one crew right left right, and Sydney can go left right left.

SYDNEY
I think Mrs. Stivers would want us to stay together.

ALEX
Well, I think it's a great idea. Who's going to go with whom?

SASHA
I will go with you, Alex.

BIRD
I'll go with the Brain!

SYDNEY
Brett? Which group do you want to go with?

BRETT
I don't know...Sydney's really really smart, but Alex seems pretty sure which way to go...

ALEX
Well?

BRETT
Don't rush me! This is an important decision. If I go with the wrong person, we could get lost in this vast museum, and never be heard from again! We're going to starve to death. Then someday, they'll find our bones in an out of the way room, picked clean by Museum Mice, and add them to the prehistoric man exhibit!

SYDNEY
There are no such things as museum mice.

BIRD
There could be...you never know...

ALEX
Oh, for heaven's sake --choose!

BRETT
I'm trying, I'm trying! Wait...what do you have in your pockets?

ALEX
Our pockets?

EACH KID SEARCHES THROUGH PANTS AND JACKET POCKETS AND PULLS OUT PROPS.

SASHA
I have my passport, three Petruskian rubles, a picture of my family, and kreplec.

BIRD
Kreplec?? What's that.

SASHA
Traditional breakfast paste from my homeland. Made of soybeans, peanut butter, goat's milk and cinnamon.

THE OTHERS REACT IN VARIOUS WAYS.

                    SYDNEY
I have my PDA, an energy bar, Capri Sun, my
          compass, my house key, and gum.

                    BIRD
I have a my favorite jellybean, a box of raisins,
          some Pokémon foil cards, and an extra
          shoelace.

                    BRETT
Alex, what do you have?

                    ALEX
The two most important tools for survival.

ALEX HOLDS UP A CREDIT CARD AND A PAGER.

                    BIRD
A credit card and a pager??

                    ALEX
It's not just a credit card. It's the Versa
          Titanium Card.

                    BRETT
Okay, I'll go with Bird and the Brain. At least
          with them I know I won't starve.

                    SASHA
Kreplec is highly nutritious and gives you energy
          for hours. Would you like to try some?

THE OTHERS REACT IN VARIOUS WAYS.

                    ALEX
Okay, let's go. You head your way, and we'll go
          the right way.

SYDNEY
Are you sure that you want to split up? I don't think it's the most prudent idea...

SASHA
Is Prudence here?

SYDNEY
No, she had the flu and couldn't come on the field trip. Why?

BIRD LAUGHS.

ALEX
Come on, Sasha. We're off to find Mrs. Stivers and the rest of the class!

SASHA
I am right behind, my captain.

THE TWO GROUPS SEPARATE, EACH STARTING TO GO THEIR OWN WAY.

SFX LOUD BUMP O.S.

THE KIDS FREEZE IN THEIR TRACKS. THEN BEGIN TO LOOK AROUND.

BIRD
(LOUD WHISPER)
What was that?

SYDNEY
(IMITATING BIRD'S LOUD WHISPER)
I don't know.

SASHA
Perhaps the Egyptian moomies are restless.

                    BRETT
          (LOOKING BACK AT THE SARCOPHAGUS)
Do...do you think so?

BIRD WALKS OFF CAMERA AND BACK AGAIN.

                    BIRD
Nah...it's not the mummies. Just the door to this
          room. It swung closed and locked us in,
          izzall.

                    BRETT
Locked in?!?

                    SYDNEY
Are you sure?

                    BIRD
Of course I'm sure!

ALEX AND SASHA CROSS TO THE DOOR AND TRY TO PUSH IT
OPEN.

                    ALEX
It won't budge.

                    SASHA
It is really stook.

                    BRETT
We're trapped, and now they'll never find us!
          We're doomed!

                    V.O.
Attention patrons: The Museum will be closing in
          half an hour.

BIRD PLAYS WITH A POKÉMON CARD.

                    SYDNEY
This is problematic.
          (NOTICING BIRD HOLDING THE CARD OVERHEAD)
What are you doing?

                    BIRD
I'm using this foil card as a reflective signal.
          I'm surprised you didn't think of it.

                    SYDNEY
There's no sun in here!

                    ALEX
Does anyone have any paper? We can write a note
          and slip it under the door.

                    SASHA
We can write it on my ruble.

                    SYDNEY
Does anyone have a pen?

THEY ALL LOOK AT EACH OTHER AND SHAKE HEADS NO.

BRETT CROSSES TO THE DOOR AND POUNDS IT.

                    BRETT
Help! We're trapped in here and we're going to be
          eaten by ferocious Museum Mice!!!

                    SASHA
Are they really ferocious?

                    ALEX
Oh, please.

                    SYDNEY
                 (TO BIRD)
What're you doing now?

BIRD
Cat's cradle.

SYDNEY
How is that going to help get us out?

BIRD
It's not, but I was getting bored.

BRETT
…walls…closing in…
(STARTS TO BREATHE IN SHORT BREATHS)
I'm...getting...asthma...

ALEX
Oh, for Pete's sake you are not.

SYDNEY
Brett's hyperventilating. Does anyone have a paper bag?

SASHA
I just have the baggy that holds my kreplec.

SYDNEY
Hand it over.

SASHA HANDS SYDNEY THE BAGGY, WHO PUTS IT TO BRETT'S MOUTH.

BRETT
...smells...weird...

SYDNEY
Just breathe into it!

BRETT BREATHES INTO THE BAG, AND STARTS TO BREATHE NORMALLY AGAIN.

BRETT
It's beginning to smell kinda good now.

BRETT TASTES THE KREPLEC. TENTATIVELY AT FIRST, THEN TAKES WHOLE FINGERFULLS OF THE STUFF.

BIRD
He can't get enough of it!

ALEX
Gimme some of that. I just realized I'm hungry, too.

THE KIDS DIG INTO THE KREPLEC.

BIRD
It's so good!

BRETT
I feel good!

SASHA
In my country we have phrase. "Stolinyavna."

ALEX
What does that mean?

SASHA
"I told you so."

SYDNEY
I feel really strong.

THE KIDS LOOK AT EACH OTHER, SUDDENLY GETTING THE SAME IDEA. THEY RUSH TO THE DOOR AND EACH WORKS TOGETHER TO PUSH IT OPEN.

                        BIRD
We did it!

                        BRETT
We're free!

                        SASHA
I see Mrs. Stivers and the class down the hall.

THEY RUN OFF THROUGH THE DOOR. BIRD HOLDS BACK.

                        BIRD
Darn. I was kinda hoping I'd see some Museum Mice.

BIRD RUNS OFF AS WE

FADE OUT.

BIRDBRAINS

Episode 2: "Bugs"

Number of Characters: 3   Running time: About 6 minutes.

Characters

BIRD

SYDNEY

COOKIE, their friend from school.

EXT: A PARK - AFTERNOON

<u>THE BIRD AND THE BRAIN ARE DISCOVERED</u> NEAR THE POND IN FRIENDSHIP PARK. SYDNEY INSPECTS AN INSECT ON A LEAF, WHILE BIRD RUNS BACK AND FORTH WAVING HANDS IN THE AIR.

BIRD

Butterfly! Flutterby! Flying high up in the sky!

SYDNEY

Will you knock that off? I'm trying to study *Coleoptera bijoux*.

BIRD

I didn't know you were taking that in summer school, too. I'm working on a science experiment for our nature class.

                    SYDNEY

Coleoptera bijoux is a jeweled beetle. Can you try to catch your butterflies more quietly?

                    BIRD

I'm not trying to catch them. I'm trying to become part of their environment so I can study them more closely. Like that lady and the monkeys.

                    SYDNEY

Apes.

                    BIRD

Bless you.

                    SYDNEY

Shouldn't you be sitting quietly in the bushes so you can study them better?

                    BIRD

I tried that, but I got a cramp. So I decided to fly like a butterfly!

DANCES AROUND AND FLUTTERS HANDS EMULATING A BUTTERFLY

So what is a jeweled beetle, anyway?

                    SYDNEY

Here, look.
<u>BIRD CROSSES TO SYDNEY.</u>

                    BIRD

Wow... It looks just like a ruby.

SYDNEY PULLS A SMALL JAR FROM BACKPACK.

SYDNEY

I'm going to add it to my collection. I already have four jeweled beetles and one giant spotted grasshopper. (STARTS TO PUT THE BEETLE IN THE JAR)

BIRD

Maybe we should contact the National Guard before it gets loose!

SYDNEY

It's not a real giant grasshopper. It's just called that. It's about two inches long.

BIRD

That doesn't sound very giant, if you ask me. <u>COOKIE, A SCHOOLMATE OF THE BIRD AND THE BRAIN, ENTERS.</u>

COOKIE

Hi, Bird. Hi, Brain. What are you guys up to?

SYDNEY

Hi, Cookie.

BIRD

Brain is rescuing a beetle and taking it home so it won't get lonely like it would out here in the wild.

SYDNEY

I hardly think that Friendship Park is considered "wild."

BIRD

It can be. Very wild.

COOKIE

How?

BIRD

(LOOKING OMINOUSLY AT THE POND) You know about the ferocious ducks in the pond, don't you?

COOKIE

I've heard about them. My brother told me.

SYDNEY

I don't see any ducks.

BIRD

Of course not. It's day time. They only come out at night...

SYDNEY

Ducks are not nocturnal. They don't come out at night!

BIRD

These ones do! They're *ferocious* ducks... and they live here, in the wild. They roam the park, searching for victims. That's why people can't come here at night.

COOKIE

(LOOKING AROUND NERVOUSLY) Are you sure that they don't come out during the day?

BIRD

Oh, they would... make no mistake... but an army of butterflies keeps them away!

SYDNEY

Bird's been learning to control the butterflies with his mental powers.

COOKIE

You have mental powers??

BIRD

I do?

SYDNEY

You do.

COOKIE

You do?

BIRD

I do.

COOKIE

What can you do?

BIRD

I can control the army of butterflies, remember? (BIRD CLOSES EYES AND TOUCHES HEAD, CONCENTRATING) Ommmmm...

COOKIE

Is something going to happen?

SYDNEY

You never know, with the Bird around.
A butterfly darts from the sky and "dive bombs" cookie.

                         COOKIE

Whoah!!!! That was cool! What else can you do.
bird opens one eye to see what happened.

                          BIRD

Well, I ---

                         SYDNEY

He can move inanimate objects with his mind.

                         COOKIE

He can?

                          BIRD

I can?

                         SYDNEY

You can.
sydney pulls out the jar holding the jeweled beetle

                          BIRD

Oh, I can...I can!

                         SYDNEY

See this red jewel?

                          BIRD

It's a ruby.

                         COOKIE

Wow....

                    SYDNEY

Bird will make it leap into the air and come to life.

                    COOKIE

No way!

                    BIRD

Way.

                    SYDNEY

Very way.
AS BIRD GOES BACK TO THE "MENTAL CONCENTRATION" POSTURE, SYDNEY OPENS THE JAR. COOKIE INSPECTS THE CONTENTS, WHICH SUDDENLY LEAP OUT!

                    COOKIE

Aaaaahhh!

COOKIE RUNS AWAY. BIRD AND THE BRAIN FALL DOWN LAUGHING.

FADE OUT.

BIRDBRAINS

Episode 3: "Pie"

Number of Characters: 2   Running time: About 5 minutes.

Characters

BIRD

SYDNEY

INT: LUNCH ROOM AT FRIENDSHIP ELEMENTARY
SYDNEY AND BIRD SIT AT A TABLE EATING LUNCH.
SYDNEY HELPS BIRD WITH MATH HOMEWORK.

BIRD

I'll never get these fractions. They're too hard.

SYDNEY

Sure you will. I'll make 'em easy for you. Okay, let's say you have a pie.

BIRD

Pie! I love pie! Gosh, I hope Mom put pie in my lunch today.
bird starts rifling through a lunch bag to see if there is some pie in there.

SYDNEY

Not that kind of a pie. A pretend pie.

BIRD

It sure is a pretend pie. There's nothing in here but an egg salad sandwich and some fig newtons. Will it work with fig newtons?

SYDNEY

No, we don't need fig newtons. We are using a pie.

BIRD

But I already told you, I don't have any pie!

SYDNEY

Not real pie. An imaginary pie!

BIRD

Mmmm... an imaginary pie... strawberry rhubarb is my favorite kind of imaginary pie.

SYDNEY

It doesn't matter what kind of pie it is.

BIRD

Maybe not to you. But strawberry rhubarb is the best kind of imaginary pie there is.

SYDNEY

Fine. It can be a strawberry rhubarb pie.

BIRD

Of course, if it were real, then I'd want it to be apple. That's my favorite.

                            SYDNEY

You just said that strawberry rhubarb was you're
favorite.

                             BIRD

That's my favorite _imaginary_ pie. My favorite _real_
pie is apple! With French vanilla ice cream on
top...

                            SYDNEY

Okay, okay. It's an apple pie.

                             BIRD

You have an apple pie? I thought we didn't have
any pie!

                            SYDNEY

Let's make it a neutral pie, okay? Let's say it's
a Boston crème pie.

                             BIRD

I don't think I've ever had a Boston crème pie
before.

                            SYDNEY

They're really good.

                             BIRD

As good as imaginary strawberry rhubarb or as good
as real apple with French vanilla ice cream on top?

                            SYDNEY

I've never had an imaginary strawberry rhubarb pie.

BIRD

Oh, you are so missing out.

SYDNEY

Look, all this talk about pies is making me really hungry and lunchtime is almost over.

BIRD

That's the best thing about imaginary strawberry rhubarb pie.
You can sneak it into class and the teacher never knows.

SYDNEY

We still have to go over these fractions!

BIRD

We can't.

SYDNEY

Why not?!?

BIRD

Because I ate all the imaginary Boston crème pie already. And we have no real pie. You were right. It was good. Not as good as imaginary strawberry rhubarb pie, though.

SYDNEY

Maybe we can make it work with your fig newtons.

BIRD

Can't.

                    SYDNEY

Why not?!?

                     BIRD

I ate those, too.

SFX: THE SCHOOL BELL RINGS.
FADE OUT.

www.ingramcontent.com/pod-product-compliance
Lightning Source LLC
LaVergne TN
LVHW041635070426
835507LV00008B/630